THE PICTURE LIFE OF
MIKHAIL GORBACHEV

THE PICTURE LIFE OF

MIKHAIL GORBACHEV

BY JANET CAULKINS

FRANKLIN WATTS
NEW YORK | LONDON | TORONTO | SYDNEY
REVISED EDITION | 1989

Photographs courtesy of:
Tass from Sovfoto: pp. 8, 34 (bottom right and left),
35 (bottom left), 39, 44, 47; Novosti from Sovfoto:
pp. 10, 23, 34 (center), Sovfoto: cover, pp. 25, 28,
34 (top and center left), 35 (top and center left,
bottom, center, top right), 50; UPI/Bettmann
Newsphotos: pp. 12, 15, 35 (center), 52; Woodfin
Camp & Associates: Wally McNamee: pp. 16, 20,
26; 34 (top right), 36 (top and bottom); AP/Wide
World Photos: p. 30; Stock, Boston: pp. 34 (center
right), 36 (center); Rothco Cartoons: pp. 41 (Carl
Simpson), 54 (Boileau-Frankfort State Journal, Ky).

Library of Congress Cataloging-in-Publication Data

Caulkins, Janet.
The picture life of Mikhail Gorbachev / Janet Caulkins. — Rev.
ed., 2nd ed.
p.   cm.
Includes index.
Summary: An illustrated biography of the leader of the Soviet
Union, including a chronology of important dates in his life and a
glossary of political words.
ISBN 0-531-10694-2
1. Gorbachev, Mikhail Sergeyevich, 1931- — Portraits,
caricatures, etc. — Juvenile literature. 2. Statesmen — Soviet Union —
Biography — Juvenile literature. [1. Gorbachev, Mikhail
Sergeyevich, 1931-   . 2. Heads of state.] I. Title.
DK290.3.G67C38   1989
947.085′4′0924 — dc19
[B]
[92]   88-39141   CIP   AC

CONTENTS

NORWAY

SWEDEN

ARCTIC OCEAN

DENMARK

Murmansk

Baltic Sea

FINLAND

Latvian SSR

Estonian SSR

Arkhangelsk

Leningrad

POLAND

Belorussian SSR

| Jan. | 15° |
| July | 60° |

Moscow ★

Ukrainian SSR

Gorki

URAL MTS.

Kiev

RUSSIAN SOVIET FEDERATED SOCIALIST REPUBLIC

Dnieper River

Moldavian SSR

Don River

Kharkov

Irtysh River

Odessa

Sverdlovsk

| Jan. | 0° |
| July | 70° |

| Jan. | 30° |
| July | 75° |

Volga River

Volgograd

Trans-Siberian Railway

Omsk

Novosibirsk

Black Sea

Stavropol

CAUCASUS MTS.

Georgian SSR

Caspian Sea

TURKEY

Armenian SSR

Kazakh SSR

Azerbaijan SSR

Turkmen SSR

Uzbek SSR

CHINA

IRAN

Tashkent

Kirghiz SSR

Tadzhik SSR

Union o

| Jan. | 30° |
| July | 75° |

Average Temps
(in degrees F

Bering Sea

PACIFIC
OCEAN

| Jan. | -40° |
| July | 55° |

Lena River

Magadan

Yakutsk

Sea of Okhotsk

Amur River

Bratsk

Khabarovsk

Lake Baikal

Irkutsk

Vladivostok

MONGOLIA

Sea of Japan

N. KOREA

JAPAN

S. KOREA

viet Socialist Republics

0   600 Miles

A MEETING
IN MOSCOW

*"I feel something very serious is afoot,
something that embraces broad sections of the people,
an awareness that we cannot go on as we are."*

Mikhail Sergeyevich Gorbachev is a man who makes changes happen. In June, 1988, a change took place in the Soviet Union that made headlines throughout the world and had Soviet citizens staring in disbelief. It was an event that would seem quite ordinary to a citizen of the United States—we call it a session of Congress. Five thousand Communist party delegates from all over the Soviet Union met in Moscow, where they shouted, argued, discussed, and questioned the policies of their government. Western reporters quoted stunned Soviet citizens: ". . . to think that people can talk so freely. It is a miracle!"

This revolutionary meeting was the brainchild of the leader of the Soviet State—Mikhail S. Gorbachev. "This

Palace of Congresses has not known such discussions, comrades, for nearly six decades," Mr. Gorbachev said at the end of four days of stormy debate. Among the most daring of his suggestions was a proposal to transfer some of the power over day-to-day life, away from the Communist party to popularly elected legislatures.

To Western nations it seems incredible that Soviet leaders would even consider such ideas. In the United States, politicians, government experts, TV commentators, and news analysts wondered just how far Mr. Gorbachev would go, and what the "new openness" and the proposed political changes within Russia would mean to the rest of the world.

Mikhail Gorbachev was already known at home and abroad as a different kind of Soviet leader. In the United States we had sampled his informal ways and forceful style as he met with President Ronald Reagan. Six months before the party meeting in Moscow, Gorbachev had come here to sign a treaty limiting nuclear arms—a treaty he called "the first step down the road to a nuclear-free world."

GORBACHEV PRESIDES AT THE 1988 PARTY CONFERENCE. A SHADOWY PORTRAIT OF LENIN LOOMS BEHIND HIM.

THE START OF SOMETHING BIG?
GENERAL SECRETARY GORBACHEV IS GREETED BY
PRESIDENT RONALD REAGAN IN WASHINGTON, D.C.

A MEETING
IN WASHINGTON

In Moscow there is a broad avenue called the Kalinin Prospect. At one end, towering above the street is a giant outdoor TV screen. On a December evening in 1987, men and women in fur hats, with their coat collars turned up, stood in the icy wind, clutching their shopping bags and briefcases. On the screen, they watched their leader, Mikhail Sergeyevich Gorbachev, shake hands with the president of the United States, half the world away, in Washington, D.C.

In the United States, Gorbachev probably arouses more intense interest than any other head of state in the world. Why is that? Because, between them, the United States and the Soviet Union have the nuclear power to destroy each other and the rest of the world as well. Now, for once, the Soviet Union and the United States need the same thing—an end to an arms race that is too expensive and dangerous for either of us. But can we "do business" with a country that Winston Churchill called "a riddle, wrapped in a mystery inside an enigma?" (An *enigma* means a mysterious riddle, and the phrase became famous because it described how very baffling the Western countries found the Soviet Union.)

So far, we have not been able to deal successfully for long with a leader from the Kremlin. Now we think and hope this man may be different from the others.

Old Enemies • Once, back in the early 1940s, during World War II, the United States and the Soviet Union were allies. Since then we have mainly viewed each other as dangerous. By the 1950s things were so bad the term *Cold War* was invented to describe our relationship. The Soviet leader Nikita Khrushchev shouted and banged his shoe on the desk at the United Nations. He scornfully told the Western nations that their systems of government were bound to fail. Communism would prevail. "We will bury you," he said. The phrase frightened and enraged many people, although Khrushchev wasn't

WAGING THE COLD WAR: IN 1960, NIKITA KHRUSHCHEV BERATED THE WESTERN NATIONS AT THE U.N. AT ONE POINT HE TOOK OFF HIS SHOE AND BANGED IT ON HIS DESK.

talking about war, but about history: in the end, he believed, *capitalism* would fail and communism would be the successful system.

In the early 1970s a more relaxed atmosphere called *détente* was soon followed by another ice age. Both countries went back to name-calling and arms build-up instead of diplomacy: Soviet leaders called us "imperialist aggressors," and President Reagan called the USSR an "evil empire," destined for "the ash heap of history." Both nations were spending billions on the technology of modern warfare and stockpiles of nuclear weapons.

Then, in 1985, the Soviets got a new leader, Mikhail Gorbachev. Two years later, while Moscow citizens gazed at that giant TV screen and thousands of U.S. reporters covered the event in Washington, President Reagan and General Secretary Gorbachev shook hands on a treaty to limit nuclear armaments. That was in early December 1987. Now, people all over the world intently follow the new relationship between these two nations.

IN THE SNOWY DARK, MOSCOW
CITIZENS WATCH AN OUTDOOR TV
TO SEE RONALD REAGAN WELCOME
GORBACHEV IN WASHINGTON, D.C.,
DECEMBER, 1987.

A New Kind of Leader • Soviet leaders since the days of Stalin have been suspicious of the West. They have been old men, without higher education, somewhat rough and unpolished—isolated from the rest of the developed world. Gorbachev is a leader from a new generation. He is younger, and well educated. (He is the first since Lenin, who led the Russian Revolution, to have a university degree.) And he has "been around." More than any other Russian leader, he has traveled—and what is more, he has traveled in the West. Gorbachev has taken a firsthand look at the Western world, and he sees the higher standards of living and productivity in developed nations outside Russia—standards that must be raised at home if his country is to prosper. He has asked the Soviet people to develop their own initiative and to use their creative energy in ways that would have previous Soviet leaders spinning in their graves. No wonder we want to know all we can about him.

UP FROM THE RANKS

We want to learn all about Mikhail Gorbachev—we *need* to know about him—but that is easier said than done. The Soviets are secretive about the lives of their leaders. Personal details are not available to reporters, at home or abroad—and the Soviet press does not have the freedom of ours to poke around, investigate, and ask questions. We do, however, know quite a lot about Gorbachev's political career, and we know something about his early life as well.

Mikhail's Childhood • Mikhail Gorbachev (pronounced gore-ba-CHAWF) was born on March 2, 1931, in the village of Privolnoye, near Stavropol in the northern Caucasus. (That is the region between the Black and Caspian seas that contains the Caucasus Mountains.) The small stone house is still there, and Gorbachev's mother and sister still live in the village. Gorbachev's family were peasants, and they were poor, but they had one important advan-

FAMILY PHOTOS: ABOVE, LITTLE MIKHAIL
WITH HIS GRANDPARENTS; BELOW, GORBACHEV
WITH RAISA AND THEIR DAUGHTER, IRINA.

tage—Gorbachev's father and grandfather were Communist party members. That was unusual. Fewer than 10 percent of Soviet adults belong to the party; membership is considered both an honor and a privilege.

Those were years when the dictator Joseph Stalin had set out to destroy the class of well-off peasants called *kulaks,* who owned their own land and ran their own small farms. The old agricultural system was broken up, the kulaks were run off their farms, or killed, and huge stocks of grain were requisitioned by Stalin. The result was the terrible famine and widespread starvation of the 1930s in which seventy-five million people died. Mikhail's grandfather, Andrei, helped organize a collective farm and his father, Sergei, drove a combine tractor for a government machine tractor station, so although they were poor, they survived. When Mikhail was eight years old, World War II began. In 1941 the German army invaded Russia. Mikhail's father fought at the front, while back home the family struggled to get enough to eat. For a while Mikhail could not go to school because he had no shoes.

The German occupation of his homeland made a deep impression on Mikhail. War losses were more terrible in Russia than in any other country; twenty million Russians had lost their lives by the time the war ended.

After the war, teenage Mikhail ("Misha" for short) spent school vacations working in the wheat fields. He drove an old-fashioned combine harvester that had no cab, so the driver was surrounded by blowing grain and chaff that made it hard to breathe. The summers were furnace-hot, and late in the harvest season the weather was numbingly cold. Combine drivers wrapped themselves in straw to keep from freezing.

The Komsomol • At that time, Mikhail also worked as an organizer with the Communist Youth League, the *Komsomol.* This was of the greatest importance to his later career. In the USSR there is only one party—the *CPSU,* the *Communist Party of the Soviet Union.* Anyone who rises to high political office must be a member of the CPSU, but you cannot simply join because you want to. You must first be sponsored by other members, and, once accepted, your membership is on a trial basis. You must demonstrate your loyalty and political reliability before you can become a full member. Most recruits to the Communist party come through the Komsomol.

It was through his work for the Komsomol that Gorbachev got his political start.

Life at the University • When he was nineteen, Mikhail took another step up the ladder. He was admitted to the law school of Moscow State University, the finest university in the Soviet Union, and very hard to get into. But Mikhail had graduated from high school with a silver

MEETING WITH SOVIET AND AMERICAN STUDENTS
IN MOSCOW. THE U.S. STUDENT GROUP, CALLED
"DIRECT CONNECTION," WANTS TO IMPROVE
RELATIONS BETWEEN THE U.S. AND THE USSR.

medal, as an excellent student, and of course his work with the Komsomol helped. Besides that, his father and grandfather had been hard-working members of the Communist party.

University students certainly did not live in the lap of luxury, however. Reporters for *Time* magazine managed to interview some of Gorbachev's fellow students about his university days (no "official" information is available). According to them, Gorbachev's first three years were spent in a cold, noisy barracks "that housed ten thousand young people packed eight or more to a room," with washrooms, but no baths or showers. Students took the metro (the subway) to classes in the law faculty where they heard lectures for six hours, Monday through Saturday. There was no cutting classes. Attendance was taken, and absence could lead to expulsion.

Raisa • It was in this student dormitory that Gorbachev met his future wife, Raisa Maksimovna. Fellow students now living outside the Soviet Union told the *Time* reporters that when Mikhail and Raisa were married, Mikhail's roommates departed temporarily so the couple could be alone together for their wedding night.

When Mikhail graduated, the couple settled back in Stavropol. They had a little girl and named her Irina. Irina must now be in her thirties. She is a doctor, married to another doctor, but we don't even know for sure what

RAISA GORBACHEV AND HER HUSBAND

Irina's married name is, although we have learned that her husband's first name is Anatoli. Since the Soviets guard personal histories as they do state secrets, it is not easy for Western reporters to confirm what details they do learn informally. We know that Irina has a daughter whose name is sometimes given as Oksana, and sometimes as Xenia or Ksenia (Ksanochka is her pet-name). She is probably about seven years old. When former president Jimmy Carter visited Moscow in 1987, Gorbachev told Carter that he had another grandchild, but he would not reveal any more details. In 1988, at the time of the summit meeting in Washington, reporters still did not know the child's sex or name!

Comrade Gorbachev • In Stavropol, Mikhail became an official of the city Komsomol, a job that led to quick promotion. He also took some correspondence courses and earned another degree—this time in agricultural economics. Gorbachev was interested in improving conditions for farmers and workers. He remembered his own hard-working days in the wheat fields—and Soviet agriculture was still suffering from old-fashioned equip-

IRINA, ANATOLI, AND
THEIR DAUGHTER OKSANA

GORBACHEV REAPS SMILES FROM FARMERS IN TASHKENT,
UZBEKISTAN, THE "ORIENT" OF THE SOVIET UNION.

ment and lack of the basic methods of modern farming. Gorbachev saw clearly that drastic changes were needed, and a career in politics seemed the best way to make them. At this time, he still had absolute faith in the system of the Communist hierarchy by which local groups carry out faithfully the orders handed down from above. He moved up steadily through the ranks of the Communist party.

At the age of forty-seven, Gorbachev became secretary for agriculture in the *Central Committee of the Communist Party.* This is a very important position. The USSR has a brief, often harsh, growing season. Most of the Soviet Union is in the same latitude as northern Canada and Alaska; only 10 percent of the land is truly arable—and there is a huge population to feed.

Because of Gorbachev's new job, the family moved to Moscow. Raisa took a position teaching political philosophy at Moscow University.

Gorbachev was good at his job. He cut through red tape and got things done—and he had a knack for doing it without getting people upset. He was smart and full of energy, and by all reports he was stubbornly honest, refusing to accept or hand out special favors, a common practice. His obvious devotion to the party and its principles added to his success, and by 1980 he was a very important man in Soviet politics. In that year he became

a full member of the all-powerful *Politburo*. He was 49—
two decades younger than the average age of the other
members of the Politburo.

The New Leader • Then, in quick succession, three el-
derly Russian heads of state died: Brezhnev, Andropov,
and finally seventy-two-year-old Konstantin Chernenko.
Gorbachev led the mourners who walked behind Chernenko's open coffin in Moscow's Red Square. It was a
solemn hour. The coffin was paraded slowly to the music
of Chopin's "Funeral March." Thousands of soldiers in
high boots and heavy fur hats stood at attention in the
snow. But the world took note of Gorbachev's special
position at the head of the mourners. It was a symbol of
his office. He was the new General Secretary of the
Soviet Union.

AS THE NEW LEADER
OF THE SOVIET UNION,
MIKHAIL GORBACHEV LED
THE MOURNERS BEHIND
THE OPEN COFFIN OF
KONSTANTIN CHERNENKO.

GORBACHEV'S COUNTRY

To understand Mikhail Gorbachev, we should try to have a clear idea of his country, for he may be a new political force, but he is no "citizen of the world"; he is a Russian patriot, Russian to the bone.

USSR stands for Union of Soviet Socialist Republics. This huge country—the largest in the world—is made up of fifteen "republics" governed by councils called Soviets. It covers one-seventh of the land area of the earth, and spans eleven time zones. Although we commonly refer to the Soviet Union as "Russia," Russia is really *in* the Soviet Union. It is the largest, most powerful of the Soviet republics—over twice the size of the United States—and its language is the official language of the USSR. Most higher education is in Russian, and almost all of the top officials in the Communist party and the Politburo are Russian. Privolnoye, where Gorbachev was born, is in the Russian republic.

The Unmelted Melting Pot • The Soviet Union also includes 170 different ethnic groups (called "nationalities"), speaking 100 different languages. Some of them live in climates of arctic cold (where the average winter temperature is minus 56° F); others live in deserts where camels are still used for transportation. The customs of these groups, and the way their people live are often centuries apart. There are dusty Muslim villages in the central Asian USSR, and European-style cities with nightclubs and rock bands on the western borders. There are nomads who roam the frozen north and Turkish tribes who survive in the harsh deserts.

According to the Soviet constitution, the ethnic groups are all entitled to education and local government in their native languages, as well as representation in national government. But all of these nationalities, with their different needs and different interests, are governed and controlled by the *Secretariat* and the *Politburo* of the Communist party in Moscow, as much as five time zones away. This is the country that Gorbachev wants to bring into the modern world—a country where he envisions many changes.

TO BUY ANYTHING, YOU STAND IN LINE . . .

GLASNOST AND PERESTROIKA

Gorbachev's country is one of the most advanced in the world in military and space technology, and it is second after the United States in industrial power. But when Gorbachev took the reins, it was also among the most backward of the industrial nations in many other ways. Gorbachev complains that Soviet rockets can fly to Venus but Soviet factories cannot seem to turn out good household appliances; 40 percent of fires in Moscow are said to be caused by defective TV sets. A pair of shoes doesn't last out the winter.

Factories are not the only problem. The Soviet Union does not grow enough food to feed its own people—in farming areas, grain is often still threshed by hand. There is not enough transportation or storage for grain and a lot of it rots, while the country buys wheat from abroad.

Once, the Soviet Union was famous for its literate, educated work force of first-class scientists and engineers. Now the education system suffers from rigid central control. Teachers in some of the Soviets have been discouraged by local authorities from failing students no matter how they deserve it; failing grades don't "look good" for the district. And the schools suffer from lack of money. According to one Soviet leader, many schools have no central heating, 30 percent lack running water, and 40 percent have no indoor toilets.

Consumer goods and services are also in short supply. It is even hard to find toothpaste in the state stores. In the cities there are long lines for food and long waiting lists for automobiles and apartments.

The Russians are a patient and patriotic people. They are known for their willingness to accept whatever their country calls on them to endure. They take hardship with resignation and humor. In Moscow, the citizens joke about the shortages and lack of services: A man puts his name on the waiting list for a car. He is told it will arrive in three years, on March 7, 1993. "Please," he begs, "change the date; I can't pick it up on March 7, the plumber is coming on that day."

But the low standard of living, lack of goods, and failing economy are no joke, and the people's patience is running out. Gorbachev knows these problems must be solved before they mean disaster for his country. "This is the only opportunity we will have," he says grimly.

THE REFRIGERATORS IN THIS SOVIET PLANT ARE
YEARS OUT OF DATE COMPARED TO U.S. MODELS.

The Bureaucracy • All these problems are caused in part by the state's strict control of every aspect of Soviet life. You have to have a permit, or approval, for whatever you plant, make, or sell; for how many people you employ and what you pay and are paid; for what supplies or parts you stock. Control is administered by an enormous, sluggish *bureaucracy.* Gorbachev wants to change all that. Many of the *bureaucrats*—the ministers and minor officials of the system—are in privileged positions; they enjoy their power and they are often the first to receive housing and cars. Many actively dislike the idea of change. They are eager to protect their own positions and privileges and their own local power. If they drag their feet they can probably ruin Gorbachev's chances for success.

Communications • Another reason for the surprising backwardness of the Russian economy is the tight control held by the government and its ministries over every form of communication. (Even the street maps people can buy have been falsified by the *KGB*.) There has been no free exchange of ideas or information. There are few office computers. Photocopying machines must be registered by the state; even the use of mimeograph machines is controlled. Under such a "closed" system, technology and know-how cannot grow or spread from one area of the economy to another.

Glasnost, the New Openness • Gorbachev's answer to these problems is, first, a policy he calls *glasnost,* or "openness." Under *glasnost* people are allowed to exchange ideas more freely; editors can say what they think; and the press has more freedom to choose what to write about. *Glasnost* extends to the arts as well. Recently the Nobel-prize-winning novel *Doctor Zhivago,* by Boris Pasternak, was published in the Soviet Union, where it had been banned since 1958.

But *glasnost* is not meant to undermine the supreme power of the Communist party. And that is one of Gorbachev's problems: to bring his country into the modern industrial world, he must make it more open and flexible, which means giving up some of the party's rigid control over every aspect of daily life. That is the risk Gorbachev asked his fellow Communists to take, at the dramatic party conference in June, 1988.

Perestroika—Restructuring • Gorbachev believes that *glasnost* is necessary to an even more important policy—*perestroika,* which means "restructuring." Gorbachev wants to restructure the economy. He wants to reduce the mountains of government regulations and required permits that have built up the bureaucracy. He wants people to complain about corrupt or lazy leaders, managers, or civil servants. He wants to make factories more efficient and raise levels of production. Manufacturers will depend on being competitive, meeting costs, and making a profit; wages and salaries will depend on profits. Factories that operate at a loss will fail instead of getting government support. Gorbachev says they will have to stop "scrounging from the state." To that end he wants to give both managers and workers freedom to use their own ideas and initiative—and be responsible for the results.

Gorbachev wants to make farms more productive, too. He would allow farmers to sell more of their own produce. And he wants to raise the level of education to meet the needs of a modernized society. He wants, in fact, to prod, push, or, if necessary, drag the Soviet Union into the world of modern industrialized nations.

But this will involve great expense and difficult changes that may not always work out as planned.

As Gorbachev admits, many people within his own country find these new ideas hard to understand. After so many years of being told exactly what to do and how to do it, they are expected to act for themselves and sink or swim on their own. Gorbachev himself says: "This is not an easy process. It is not without pain. We still often scare one another."

PERSUADING WORKERS THAT *PERESTROIKA* WILL WORK

A HORSE OF A
DIFFERENT COLOR

Mikhail Gorbachev is the youngest person ever to lead the Soviet state—nineteen years younger than was the last leader, Konstantin Chernenko, and twenty years younger than U.S. president Ronald Reagan. Other than the steps of his political career, we have few "official" personal details. We know that Gorbachev is very active and health-conscious. He takes long walks, doesn't smoke, and drinks only moderately. He is a "workaholic" and he reads a lot, including foreign writers in translations. At school he liked math and science, history and literature. He has written several books.

But what kind of man is he? We usually form a picture of an important politician through a flood of personal material, issued officially or dug up by reporters or volunteered by friends (and sometimes by enemies). It seems incredible to Americans that so little is known, even to Soviet citizens, about people in public life in the USSR. When a previous leader, Yuri Andropov, died, his wife was seen at the funeral; until then few people abroad or even at home had known he was married!

So Gorbachev himself has been a mystery man to us. We only know what we can observe through our own experience. By now, a number of Americans have met him personally. Members of Congress and politicians, writers and artists, business people and military people have had a chance to talk with him. Some of these people still view the Soviet Union with the greatest suspicion, and are wary of Gorbachev's motives. Others are eager to abandon the Cold War, and wish him well. But every one of them recites the same list of qualities that make Mr. Gorbachev a leader who stands out: mental toughness, directness, and self-confidence head the list. All are impressed with his willingness to address hard problems, his realistic attitude, the depth and breadth of his information, and his ability to think on his feet.

Some other qualities stand out. Gorbachev is impatient with red tape and hates formality—we know that because we have seen it. When he visited Canada and England in 1983 and 1984, he startled everyone: he didn't stand around stiffly at formal receptions. He visited farms and factories. He talked informally with all kinds of people. He does that at home, too. In a book he wrote explaining his new policy of *perestroika,* he says that he has been accused by politicians in the USSR of "wooing the people," but, he says, "There are no hints,

GOING "STRAIGHT TO THE PEOPLE."
GORBACHEV LIKES TO MEET WITH PEOPLE INFORMALLY.

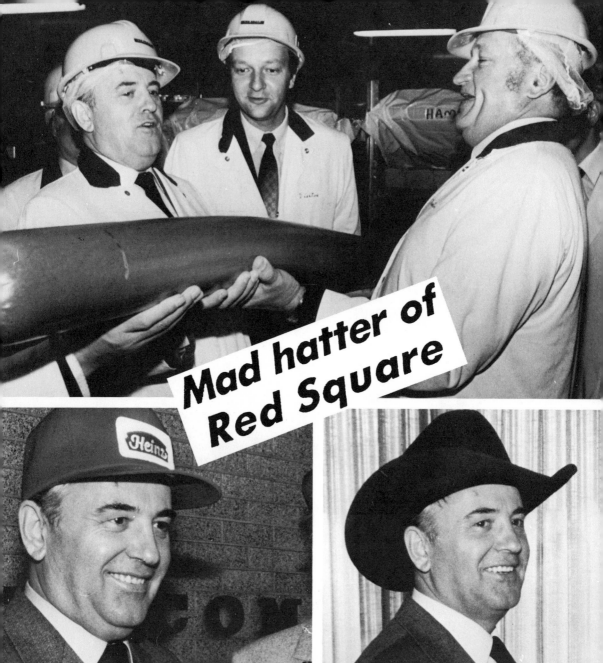

Mad hatter of Red Square

recommendations or warnings that are more valuable than those you get straight from the people." That is an unusual thought in a society where all the power flows from the top down.

And Gorbachev has charm and humor as well. A Russian politician who would wear funny hats and pose with an oversized sausage is not what Westerners had learned to expect.

The Popular "Mr. G." • In 1984 in London Gorbachev conferred with Prime Minister Margaret Thatcher in an open, friendly manner and in such reasonable terms that she was quoted around the world as saying, "I like Mr. Gorbachev; we can do business together." The British press took to calling him "Mr. G."

By the time Mr. Gorbachev arrived in Washington, we knew he was not the typical Soviet leader. In a motorcade in Washington, Mr. Gorbachev abruptly had his driver stop the big bulletproof ZIL limousine that had

THE MANY HATS OF MR. GORBACHEV: CLOWNING FOR THE CANADIAN PRESS IN 1983. *TOP:* HE HOLDS A GIANT BOLOGNA; *LEFT:* AT A KETCHUP FACTORY; *RIGHT:* AT A BARBECUE.

"I WANT TO SAY HELLO!"
IN WASHINGTON, GORBACHEV JUMPED OUT OF
HIS LIMOUSINE TO GREET PEOPLE IN THE CROWD.
BEHIND HIM A SECURITY MAN LOOKS ALARMED.

been brought over from Russia. Then Gorbachev jumped out under the alarmed noses of American secret service agents, who shouted to bystanders "Get your hands out of your pockets!" Gorbachev promptly reached into the delighted crowd to shake those hands. "I want to say hello!" he told them. KGB officers in the leading limos suddenly realized that their chief was no longer with them, and had to go speeding backward along Connecticut Avenue to find him. Headlines proclaimed, "Gorby Wins Hearts in America!" Image-conscious Americans called him a "public relations genius." A Gallup poll found Mr. Gorbachev on the list of the ten men, worldwide, most admired by Americans. Americans were amazed to meet a Soviet leader so much like us—or the way we think of ourselves—friendly, informal, humorous, and reasonable.

Iron Teeth • We have also seen another side to Mr. Gorbachev: we have seen him angry. At a meeting of publishers and journalists, when people persisted in asking him questions about human rights in the Soviet Union, Mr. Gorbachev exploded. The editor of a news magazine reports that he pounded on the table: "We shall not tolerate anyone's attempts to teach us lessons!" We are reminded that Andrei Gromyko (then foreign minister) once said of Gorbachev admiringly: "This man has a nice smile, but he has iron teeth."

VIETNAM IS MISSPELLED IN THE BANNER OF THESE
AFGHANI PROTESTERS, BUT THE IDEA IS CLEAR.
THE USSR OCCUPIED AFGHANISTAN IN 1979. UNDER
GORBACHEV, RUSSIA BEGAN TO WITHDRAW ITS TROOPS.

Gorbachev's Politics • We know that Gorbachev is a dedicated Communist—he says so. We know that in the Soviet Union he is against many of the freedoms we take for granted—he says that, too. He believes that "democracy without limits is anarchy." Under the Soviet system everyone is expected to work for the good of all; that is the key to the survival of the system. Gorbachev has made it plain that freedom of speech and assembly and freedom of the press are to be used in the service of the socialist state. Competing political parties are out, even under *glasnost*. He has not yet come to grips with problems of human rights.

Some of Gorbachev's ideas have come a long way from the old *party line*, however. He no longer believes, as Khrushchev did, that Communism is bound to take over the world. "Surely," he says, "we can be competitors without being enemies." To his own people Gorbachev says, "We must analyze not only our successes, but also our mistakes." Among the "mistakes" he lists are Soviet intervention in Poland and the invasion of Afghanistan in 1979. He also says the negative Soviet position on the United Nations has been wrong. He has even proposed a wider role for the U.N. and the International Court of Justice to decide international disputes. General Secretary Gorbachev would be an unusual politician in any country. He will have an important place in tomorrow's history books.

THE FUTURE

The changes Gorbachev wants to make in the Soviet Union are revolutionary. He must encourage and train his huge unwieldy nation to jump through the hoop of reform, changing the most basic habits of generations of citizens. Meanwhile the people are waiting skeptically for results. If *perestroika* doesn't soon raise the standard of living and set the economy on the road to health, the party will kick him out.

To carry out his plans at home, Gorbachev needs and wants something that we want, too: a less dangerous world with more normal relationships among nations. He needs money to carry out his reforms, and, for now, even the military officials of the USSR agree that pouring money into what Gorbachev calls "mountains of weapons" is something the Soviet Union just cannot afford.

This new and different Soviet leader describes the nations of the world as mountain climbers on one rope. He says, "We can either climb together or fall together into the abyss."

IMPORTANT DATES

1931   Born March 2, in village of Privolnoye in Stavropol region.

1942   German army occupies Stavropol (then called Voroshilovsk).

1940s   After the war, as a teenager, Gorbachev works at a local machine tractor station during school vacations. Becomes a member of the Komsomol (Communist Youth League).

1950   Enrolls in the law school of Moscow State University.

1952   Becomes a Komsomol organizer at the University of Moscow law school and joins the Communist party.

1955   Graduates from the University of Moscow with a law degree.

1950s and 1960s   Meets and marries Raisa Maksimovna. Returns to Stavropol and continues career in the party organization.

Daughter Irina is born.

Takes correspondence and evening courses in agronomy.

1967   Receives a degree in agricultural economics.

1970   Named first secretary of the regional organization of the Communist party (a job roughly equivalent to governor of an area of 2.4 million people).

1971   Joins the Central Committee.

1974   Elected chairman of the Youth Affairs Commission of the Supreme Soviet.

1970s   Heads delegations to Belgium and West Germany.

1978   Called to Moscow as party secretary for agriculture on the Central Committee.

1979   Becomes candidate member of the Politburo.

1980   Becomes full member of the Politburo (eight years younger than the next youngest member).

1981   Awarded the Order of Lenin "for great services to the party and the State."

1982   Soviet president Leonid Brezhnev dies at age seventy-six. Yuri Andropov, sixty-eight, named as Brezhnev's successor.

1984   Gorbachev heads delegation on a visit to Canada.

1984   Death of Andropov. Konstantin Chernenko, seventy-two, named as new general secretary of the Soviet Union.

1984   Gorbachev visits Great Britain and appears before Parliament's foreign relations committee.

1985   Death of Chernenko. Gorbachev, fifty-four, named as new general secretary of the Communist party and leader of the Soviet Union.

1986   Gorbachev and President Reagan meet at Reykjavik to talk about arms issues and to set up a possible summit meeting in the United States.

1987   December summit meeting between President Reagan and General Secretary Gorbachev to sign the INF Treaty, limiting certain intermediate-range nuclear forces.

1988   Summit meeting in Moscow between President Reagan and Gorbachev for further talks on arms limitations.

The Nineteenth All-Union Party Conference (the first since 1941) to discuss *perestroika*.

Soviet withdrawal from Afghanistan, which it had occupied by force in 1979.

The office of the presidency of the Soviet Union is given broad new powers in the fields of domestic, foreign, and national security policy.

October: The Supreme Soviet confirms Communist party General Secretary Gorbachev as president of the Soviet Union.

GLOSSARY

Bureaucracy: A rigid structure of government departments and bureaus ranked one above another; an excess of red tape and routine.

Bureaucrats: The officials in charge of the divisions of a bureaucracy.

Capitalism: An economic system in which trade, land, and industry are controlled by private owners, and in which prices, production, and distribution of goods are set mainly by the action of the free market, rather than regulation by the state.

Central Committee of the Communist Party: Several hundred members, chosen from people elected by Communist party organizations across the country. The Central Committee elects the members of the Politburo and the Secretariat.

Cold War: The hostility and distrust between the Soviet Union and the Western nations, especially during the 1950s and 1960s.

CPSU: Communist party of the Soviet Union; the party that governs the USSR. There is no other political party.

Détente: An easing of tense relations between nations.

General Secretary: The most powerful person within the Communist party. The general secretary is chairman of the Politburo and the Secretariat. Mikhail Gorbachev is now the general secretary.

Glasnost: Reduction of censorship; a Russian word, literally meaning "openness." See *Perestroika*.

Imperialism: The practice of conquering other countries, trying to control weaker countries, and forming colonies in other lands.

KGB: The state security police of the USSR.

Komsomol: The Communist Youth League; the youth organization run by the Communist party for ages fourteen to twenty-eight, in preparation for joining the Communist party.

Kulaks: A class of comparatively well-off peasants who, Stalin thought, stood in the way of collective farming in the 1930s.

Party line: The set policy of a political party; the official policies of the Communist party.

Perestroika: A Russian word meaning "reorganization," or "restructuring." *Glasnost* and *perestroika* are the means by which Gorbachev plans to change society and rebuild the economy in the USSR.

Politburo: The most powerful group in the Communist party. It sets the overall policy for the Soviet Union.

Secretariat: One of the two top groups in the Communist party of the Soviet Union (the other is the Politburo). The Secretariat is in charge of the day-to-day affairs of the Soviet Union. Together, the Secretariat and the Politburo run the country.

Supreme Soviet: The Soviet parliament, elected by all Soviet citizens over eighteen. All candidates are approved by the Communist party, and there is only one candidate for each position.

INDEX